P9-AQF-074

# How To Convince Your Parents You Can...

# Care For A Pet Guinea Pig

Stephanie Bearce

## Mitchell Lane

### PUBLISHERS

P.O. Box 196
Hockessin, Delaware 19707
Visit us on the web: www.mitchelllane.com
Comments? email us: mitchelllane@mitchelllane.com

# Mitchell Lane
## PUBLISHERS

Printing          1        2        3        4        5        6        7        8        9

### A Robbie Reader/How to Convince Your Parents You Can...

| | |
|---|---|
| Care for a Kitten | Care for a Pet Mouse |
| Care for a Pet Bunny | Care for a Pet Parrot |
| Care for a Pet Chameleon | Care for a Pet Racing Pigeon |
| Care for a Pet Chimpanzee | Care for a Pet Snake |
| Care for a Pet Chinchilla | Care for a Pet Sugar Glider |
| Care for a Pet Ferret | Care for a Pet Tarantula |
| **Care for a Pet Guinea Pig** | Care for a Pet Wolfdog |
| Care for a Pet Hamster | Care for a Potbellied Pig |
| Care for a Pet Hedgehog | Care for a Puppy |
| Care for a Pet Horse | Care for a Wild Chincoteague Pony |

Library of Congress Cataloging-in-Publication Data
Bearce, Stephanie.
  Care for a pet guinea pig / by Stephanie Bearce.
     p. cm. — (A Robbie reader. How to convince your parents you can...)
  Includes bibliographical references and index.
  ISBN 978-1-58415-797-7 (library bound)
  1. Guinea pigs as pets—Juvenile literature. I. Title. II. Title: How to convince your parents you can—care for a pet guinea pig.
  SF459.G9B424 2010
  636.935'92—dc22
                                                                    2009027350

ABOUT THE AUTHOR: Stephanie Bearce always loved animals. Her dad was a biology teacher, so she grew up with all kinds of pets. She had everything from snakes and salamanders to hamsters, gerbils, and guinea pigs. When she got older, she decided to study plants and animals. She received a degree in agriculture from Kansas State University. Then she became a science teacher. Like her dad's, her classroom was a home to all kinds of critters. She believes pets are a great way for children to learn about the world around them.

PUBLISHER'S NOTE: The facts on which this story is based have been thoroughly researched. Documentation of such research is listed on page 29. While every possible effort has been made to ensure accuracy, the publisher will not assume liability for damages caused by inaccuracies in the data, and makes no warranty on the accuracy of the information contained herein.

PLB

# TABLE OF CONTENTS

Words in **bold** type can be found in the glossary.

Bright-eyed and friendly, a guinea pig can make a great family pet.

 **Chapter One 1**

# A FURRY FRIEND

Would you like a pet that can whistle, chatter, and cuddle? Do you like cute furry animals? If so, a guinea pig may be the perfect pet for you.

Guinea pigs don't cost a lot. Often you can adopt one for a small fee. They eat pellets and vegetables, so they are not as expensive to feed as dogs or cats. Their favorite toys are cardboard and wood. They enjoy playing with people.

Guinea pigs are curious and like to explore. They want to know everything about their home—and their owners. Guinea pigs love to be petted, and they even like to sleep on laps. With their big eyes, small ears, and pig-shaped bodies, they are also very cute.

If you get a guinea pig, you will have a fun, furry friend. You can use a soft brush on your guinea pig's fur. You can make toys for it. You can even teach it to come when you call.

Guinea pigs have a good sense of hearing. They can learn that the sound of a refrigerator door means a snack is coming. They know the voices of people they like. Your guinea pig may chirp and whistle when you come home from school.

Scientists think that guinea pigs' good ears have helped them learn how to make many different sounds. They chirp, squeak, whistle, squeal, and **churr.** They also make sounds with their teeth such as grinding and chattering. Guinea pigs like to talk to each other and to their owners.

A great thing about guinea pigs is that they like to be held. Dogs and cats often grow too large to sit on a person's lap. Snakes and lizards don't like to be petted. Guinea pigs love attention. They are social animals that do not usually bite people.

You can learn to understand guinea pigs by watching how they move. When a guinea pig is happy, it jumps in the air. If a guinea pig is stretched out, it is

Baby guinea pigs are called pups. They need to stay with their mothers until they are at least six weeks old.

relaxed. Guinea pigs greet each other by bumping noses. If they are scared, they make their legs stiff and they freeze in place.

Guinea pigs are interesting animals, and they make awesome pets.

In parts of South America, guinea pigs are kept in small herds. The females are called sows, and the males are called boars.

# Chapter Two

# ALL ABOUT GUINEA PIGS

Don't be fooled by the guinea pig's name! Guinea pigs don't come from the country of Guinea. They are not pigs. And even though scientists use the name *Cavia porcellus*, which is Latin for "little pig," guinea pigs aren't related to the pig family. It is a mystery how the guinea pig got its name, but there are a lot of ideas. One is that the name comes from an old English coin called a guinea, because that is how much the animals cost. That idea is wrong, because guinea pigs got their name before the coin was invented! As for the "pig" part of their name, maybe it was given because some people thought guinea pigs looked and sounded like tiny pigs, with their round rumps, long bodies, short legs, and squeaky voices. People who like guinea pigs call them pigs, piggies, oinkers, and weekers. Guinea pigs are also sometimes called cavies (KAA-veez).

Guinea pigs are part of the **rodent** family. Their closest relatives are mice, hamsters, and squirrels.

Rodents are **mammals**. They have hair and feed their babies milk. Rodents also have gnawing teeth that never stop growing. Guinea pigs spend a lot of time eating grass, hay, and vegetables. Their teeth would get worn to nothing if they did not keep growing.

## fun**FACTS**

Guinea pigs play dead to fool other animals. If a guinea pig is scared, it will lie still and pretend to be dead. It will stay like that until the other animal gets bored and goes away.

Scientists have found fossils of animals like guinea pigs in Venezuela (veh-neh-ZWAY-luh), a country at the top of South America. The animals were as big as buffaloes and lived six million years ago in grassy marshes. Like today's guinea pigs, they had fur and small ears. Unlike today's guinea pigs, they had tails, which might have helped them balance when they stood on their back legs to look for **predators** (PREH-duh-turs).

Guinea pigs were **domesticated** (doh-MES-tih-kay-ted) for their meat and fur thousands of years ago by Inca people living in the Andes, which are mountains and highlands along the west coast of South America. Many families there still raise and eat

guinea pigs. The animals are allowed to roam freely in their houses, and they are fed table scraps.

Wild guinea pigs can be found in many parts of South America. They live in small groups and eat grasses and other plants. When they want to hide, they use the **burrows** of other animals or dig their own. They also hide in underbrush or cracks in rocks. They run in single file. They are active at night, when it is hard for predators—like hawks, snakes, and coyotes—to spot them.

In the 1500s, Europeans sailed to South America. They brought home guinea pigs, and people kept them as pets. When Queen Elizabeth I got a guinea pig, all the ladies at court wanted one. They carried their guinea pigs on silk pillows. They tried to **breed** guinea pigs with long hair and special colors.

People brought guinea pigs to the United States in the 1900s. Thirteen breeds are now recognized in the United States. They range from the popular American, with its sleek coat, to the Texel, with its long, curly hair. Another popular breed is the Abyssinian, which has a coat with swirls, called rosettes. The Peruvian has a long sweep of hair that covers its face.

Guinea pigs come in a wide variety of colors. They can be brown, black, or orange. They can be spotted, patchy, or one solid color. The agouti has

# 8 Common Types of Guinea Pigs

Abyssinian

American

Coronet

Peruvian

Silkie Sheltie

Teddy

Texel

Crested

Albino guinea pigs are all white with pink eyes. They do not have any pigment, or color, in their skin.

dark and light colors on each hair. The albino is white, with pink eyes. The Himalayan has a white body and dark nose, ears, and feet.

Guinea pigs have big, shiny eyes and blunt snouts. They have three toes on their back feet and four toes on their front feet. They do not have tails.

No matter what you call them, guinea pigs are fun pets.

Exotics veterinarians give guinea pigs checkups and can treat them for illnesses.

# Chapter Three

# FINDING THE BEST PET YET

There are many places you can get a guinea pig, including animal shelters and rescue groups. Lots of parents bring guinea pigs to shelters and rescues after their kids get tired of taking care of them. Some people lose their jobs and can no longer afford to take care of their guinea pigs. Other places you can find them are in ads in the back of the newspaper. You can also search guinea pig adoption networks on the internet. Adoption is a great way to help a guinea pig.

It is important to pick a healthy pet. Look closely at the guinea pig. The eyes should be bright and shiny. The ears should be clean. Look at the guinea pig's feet to make sure they do not have sores. The guinea pig should smell sweet and healthy.

Open the guinea pig's mouth. Make sure the teeth are shiny and white. They should not be yellow or overgrown. Check the cage for diarrhea (dy-uh-REE-uh), which is soft, runny poop. This means the

animal is sick. Look for firm, pellet-shaped poops.

There are many colors and breeds of guinea pigs. You have to decide the type you like best, but keep in mind that a guinea pig's **personality** (pur-son-AL-uh-tee) is more important than its looks.

Some guinea pigs have long hair. They are cute, but they also need to be **groomed** with a comb or brush every day. Short-haired guinea pigs do not need to be brushed.

You may want a girl (female) guinea pig, or you may want a boy (male). Both kinds are fun. Don't put a female and a male in the same cage, however, because they will have babies. You may not be able to find good homes for all of them.

Guinea pigs are happiest when they have company, so consider getting two males or two females. It is not true that male guinea pigs can't live together. They just can't live together when there is a female guinea pig nearby.

Guinea pig owners can have fun creating hiding places for their pets. These guinea pigs have their own town.

Be sure to get a guinea pig that likes to be held. Most guinea pigs love to be with people. Some are friendlier than others. Ask to hold the guinea pig. Pet it and let it get to know you. Pick the guinea pig that is best for you.

Before you bring your guinea pig home, find an **exotics veterinarian** (ek-SAH-tiks vet-ruh-NAYR-ee-un) who treats guinea pigs. Then you'll know where to go in case of an emergency.

This cube and Coroplast cage gives guinea pigs plenty of room to play, and provides good air circulation.

# Chapter Four

# HOME SWEET HOME

Your new guinea pig will need a cage. For one guinea pig, the cage should be at least two feet by two feet. Get a larger cage if you plan on keeping two guinea pigs. They will need room to play, buck, run fast, and get away from each other when they feel like it.

Choose a cage with a solid floor. Guinea pigs should not be kept in cages with wire-mesh bottoms, which can hurt their feet. Wire siding will give your guinea pig plenty of air. You can make a great cage for less than it costs to buy a small one at a pet store. Check the Internet for plans on how to build a C&C (cubes and Coroplast [KOR-oh-plast]) guinea pig cage. If you keep your C&C cage on a table, attach a cube bottom to the cube sides before you insert the Coroplast lining. Keeping the cage on a table makes it easier to care for—and easier to enjoy your guinea pigs. Never use an enclosed plastic cage or an aquarium.

Put bedding in the cage. Some people use shredded-paper bedding made for small animals. Others use kiln-dried pine shavings or aspen shavings. Never use cedar shavings. They are bad for guinea pigs.

Line the cage with newspaper, and then cover it with a thick layer of bedding. The bedding soaks up urine (YUR-in), or pee. Remove the dirtiest bedding every two or three days. About once a week, change all of the bedding.

Guinea pigs like to hide inside their cages. A clay flowerpot tipped on its side makes a good hideout. A small box made from untreated wood works, too. Be sure it has a wide doorway and is large enough for the guinea pig to turn around in. Never give your guinea pig a house made from anything **toxic** (TOK-sik), like varnished or painted wood. Guinea pigs love to chew, and varnish and paint can make them sick.

Your guinea pig needs a water bottle. Don't use a bowl because the water will get dirty. Get a water bottle with a metal tip that your guinea pig can't chew. Change the water every day, and don't put vitamins in it.

Buy a ceramic food dish that your guinea pig cannot flip over. Make sure the sides are low, so your guinea pig can reach its food.

Guinea pigs are vegetarians (veh-jeh-TAYR-ee-ins), which means they eat only plants. They need a

Like all rodents, a guinea pig's teeth are always growing. They need to chew on wooden objects to stay healthy.

daily serving of pellets made just for them. Guinea pig pellets contain **vitamin** (VY-tuh-min) C, which they need to stay healthy. Look for fresh, timothy-hay-based pellets that don't contain seeds, nuts, and other extras. Do not use rabbit food!

Give your guinea pig greens and vegetables like romaine lettuce (not iceberg), broccoli, kale, dandelion greens, parsley, tomatoes (but not the stalks or leaves), green and red bell peppers, carrots, carrot tops, watercress, beet greens, and turnip greens. You can pick dandelion greens, common grass, and clover from your lawn as long as it isn't sprayed with

**pesticides** (PES-tih-syds) or next to a busy road with lots of exhaust fumes.

Small amounts of fruit like apples, oranges, watermelon, and strawberries are also good for your guinea pig. Wash fruits and vegetables before you feed them to your guinea pig, and remove leftover fresh food after a day so that it doesn't rot in the cage.

Your adult guinea pig needs timothy hay, which is also called grass hay. Timothy hay is an important source of fiber. It also keeps your guinea pig's teeth from growing too long. Get the freshest timothy hay

Guinea pigs love fresh fruits and vegetables. Most of their diet should be pellets, but spinach is a great treat for your pet, too.

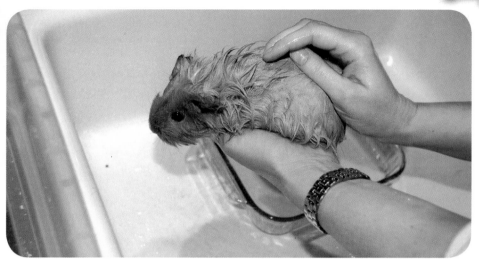

Your guinea pig should have a bath every three to four months. Use a shallow bowl of water that it can stand in, and have plenty of towels handy.

you can find, and give your guinea pig as much as it wants. Alfalfa hay should be given to baby guinea pigs and to nursing mothers.

Guinea pigs have two kinds of poop, and they eat one of those kinds. After a guinea pig eats, its food breaks down into vitamins. Some of those vitamins come out in the softer, squishier kind of poop. This is the kind you may see your guinea pig eating. Do not stop it. It helps your guinea pig **digest** (dy-JEST) its food and get vitamins back into its body.

If your guinea pig gets dirty, give it a bath with shampoo made for small animals. Clip its nails when they get too long. Don't cut into the quick! If your guinea pig gets sick, take it to an exotics veterinarian right away.

Guinea pigs like to be petted and held. Remember to keep one hand under its chest, and the other under its rump.

# Chapter Five

# ARE YOU READY FOR A GUINEA PIG?

Owning a guinea pig is a big responsibility. A guinea pig cannot fill its own water bottle, clean its own cage, or buy its own food. You must take care of your guinea pig, even on days when you don't feel like it.

Make sure that your home is safe for your guinea pig, and always keep an eye on it when it is out of its cage. Other pets you may have, such as a cat or a dog, might want to hunt your guinea pig, so don't let them near it. Do not let your piggie chew on cords. It can get shocked or killed. Do not let it gnaw on houseplants or painted wood. Don't let it climb under cabinets or through holes in the wall—it might get stuck. Don't let in fall down stairs or off furniture.

Find a safe spot for your guinea pig's cage. Choose a quiet room that isn't drafty or too hot or cold. If it's comfortable for you, it will be comfortable for your guinea pig. The room shouldn't be damp, like a laundry room or a bathroom. Your bedroom, a quiet

corner in the living room, or a heated basement may be good places. Don't put the cage next to a heat source, because guinea pigs get overheated fast. The cage should be in a bright room, but not in direct sunlight.

Put fun items in your guinea pig's cage. A clean brick laid on its side is a good place for your guinea pig to stand or stretch out. A five-inch piece of PVC pipe is a perfect hidey-hole. A cardboard box makes a fun chew toy. So do branches cut from fruit trees that are not sprayed with pesticides.

Guinea pigs enjoy exploring outdoors and sampling plants. They need close supervision to keep them safe.

If your lawn isn't chemically treated or close to a busy road and exhaust fumes, you can take your guinea pig outside in the summer. Make a temporary pen out of wire. Be sure the ground is dry and free of animal urine or poop. Give your guinea pig a place to hide and get out of the sun, like a box turned on its side. You cannot leave

**funFACTS**

Guinea pigs have a hard time judging heights. Never leave your guinea pig alone on a high place, because it may jump off and get hurt or killed.

your guinea pig alone when it is outside, so bring a good book or some homework—and keep an eye out for cats and dogs.

Cuddle your guinea pig every day. Let your guinea pig out of its cage to run on the floor for at least twenty minutes a day. If you do not, your guinea pig could get sick from lack of exercise.

If you know you are ready to have a pet, talk to your family and make sure they want one, too. A pet is fun for everyone, but it is also work for everyone. If you are sick or leave home, someone else will need to care for your guinea pig.

Tell your parents that you will give your guinea pig food and water every day. Tell them you will keep

If you have more than one guinea pig, you can share the fun with family and friends.

its cage clean. Tell them you will give it exercise and attention. But only tell them if it is the truth! If you have a pet, you must do the work.

If you get a guinea pig, you will get to spend lots of time with a cuddly, furry friend. You will have lots of fun together.

# FIND OUT MORE

## Books

Birmelin, Immanuel. *My Guinea Pig and Me.* Hauppauge, NY: Barron's Educational Series Inc., 2001.

Elward, Margaret, and Mette Ruelokke. *Guinea Piglopaedia: A Complete Guide to Guinea Pig Care.* Surrey, England: Ringpress Books, 2004.

Vanderlip, Sharon L., D.V.M. *The Guinea Pig Handbook.* Hauppauge, NY: Barron's Educational Series, Inc., 2003.

## Works Consulted

Altman, Dietrich. *Guinea Pigs.* London: Blanford Books, 1997.

Barrie, Anmarie. *A Step by Step Book About Guinea Pigs.* Neptune City, NJ: T.F.H. Publications, Inc., 1987, 1994.

Guidry, Virginia Parker. *Guinea Pigs: Practical Advice to Caring for Your Guinea Pig.* Irvine, CA: Bowtie Press, 2004.

Gurney, Peter. *The Proper Care of Guinea Pigs.* Neptune City, NJ: T.F.H. Publications, Inc., 1999.

Mancini, Julie. *Guinea Pigs.* Neptune City, NJ: T.F.H. Publications, Inc., 2006.

Sigler, Dale. *A Grown-Up's Guide to Guinea Pigs.* Lincoln, NE: IUniverse.com, Inc., 2000.

Siino, Betsy Sikora, consulting editor. *The Essential Guinea Pig.* New York: Howell Book House, 1998.

## Web Addresses

The British Broadcasting Corporation—Pets
http://www.bbc.co.uk/nature/animals/pets/guinea_pig.shtml

Cavy Cages: How to Make a C&C Cage
http://www.guineapigcages.com/howto.htm

Cavy Cages: Your Guinea Pig's Home
http://www.guineapigcages.com/

Cavy Madness: Making the World a Nicer Place . . . One Guinea Pig at a Time
http://www.cavymadness.com/index.html

# FIND OUT MORE

Guinea Lynx: Medical and Care Guide for Guinea Pigs
   http://www.guinealynx.info/
Guinea Pig Club
   http://www.guineapigsclub.com/
Guinea Pig Compendium
   http://www.aracnet.com/~seagull/Guineas/
The Humane Society of the United States
   http://www.hsus.org/pets/pet_care/rabbit_horse_and_other_pet_
   care/how_to_care_for_guinea_pigs.html
Metropolitan Guinea Pig Rescue: What to Feed Your Guinea Pig
   http://www.mgpr.org/MGPR/Guinea%20Pig%20Diet.htm
Pigloo: A Rescue-Friendly Guinea Pig Community
   http://pigloo.net/

**Rescues and Adoption Networks**
Cavy Spirit
   http://www.cavyspirit.com/
The Critter Connection, Inc.
   http://www.petfinder.com/shelters/CT208.html
Guinea Pig Adoption Network
   http://www.gpan.net/index.html
Guinea Pig Home
   http://www.guineapighome.com/
Metropolitan Guinea Pig Rescue
   http://www.mgpr.org/
Texas Rustlers Guinea Pig Rescue
   http://theguineapigrescue.com/index.htm

# GLOSSARY

**breed**—A particular type of an animal; also, to put animals together so that they can have babies, especially when whoever puts them together is hoping the babies will have the preferred traits, such as fur length or colors, of their parents.

**burrows** (BUR-ohz)—Holes or tunnels dug as living space.

**churr** (CHUR)—To make a vibrating, whirring sound.

**digest** (dy-JEST)—To break down food (in the body).

**domesticated** (doh-MES-tih-kay-ted)—Made tame.

**exotics veterinarian** (ek-SAH-tiks vet-ruh-NAYR-ee-un)—An animal doctor who knows how to treat unusual pets, such as guinea pigs.

**groom** (GROOM)—To care for the animal's hair and nails.

**mammal** (MAA-mal)—An animal that has hair or fur, feeds the babies their mother's milk, and has a backbone.

**personality** (pur-son-AL-uh-tee)—The qualities that make one person, animal, or thing distinct from another.

**pesticides** (PES-tih-syds)—Chemicals used to kill pests on plants.

**predator** (PREH-duh-tur)—An animal that hunts other animals for food.

**rodent** (ROH-dent)—A type of mammal whose front teeth continue to grow; rodents must gnaw on things to keep their teeth from growing too long.

**toxic** (TOK-sik)—Something that contains a poison.

**vitamin** (VY-tuh-min)—A nutrient necessary to the body's health.

# INDEX